# Introduction

A quick search on Google reveals 250,000,000 results for Internet dating. What was once a bit of a guilty secret that we kept hidden from our friends, families and colleagues is now a very socially acceptable way to meet people, and consequently we are awash with options to help us find love in cyberspace.

There are approximately 14.2 million single people in the UK at the moment, and the number of Internet dating websites launching each week in this country is testament to the fact that this phenomenon is here to stay.

Internet dating is huge and growing every day. With so many of us living life in the fast lane, finding love online could seem like the best, easiest and quickest way to meet new people. We live in a high-tech age of instant and constant access to information, and the way we want to meet people and have relationships is also starting to change.

Internet dating is easy, quick and the choice of different websites is enormous. However, before you hand over your hard-earned cash to some dot com entrepreneur and get carried away with promises of finding your soulmate or love of your life online, there are a few things that you need to consider. Internet dating can be a fun, refreshing and fascinating way to meet new people, but it can also be disappointing, upsetting and awkward. We hope this guide will help you date safely, have fun and know when things are not working out and when to move on.

Internet dating might be something that you have always wanted to try but you have never been quite brave enough to fill in your profile and start searching. It is now a tried and tested method of meeting Mr or Miss Right, and many couples who have met in cyberspace have gone on to have fully functional relationships, get married and have a family.

Of course, with every good news story there comes a flurry of cautionary tales from people who have not had positive experiences and regret having ever signed up to a dating website in the first place. The key to successful Internet dating is to treat each and every date as just that – a date. It is unlikely that the first person who shows any interest in you is likely to be the love of your life.

Long and drawn-out email or instant messenger chats are all very well, but all the experts agree that we know if we like someone new within a few minutes or even seconds of being in their company.

Dragging out the first date will not necessarily mean you know each other really well before you meet – the harsh reality is that you probably won't know each other at all, as we can be whoever we choose on the Internet.

Keeping people hanging on for weeks and weeks and making promises of forthcoming dates gives people false hope and is not good practice. Instead, if someone catches your eye and they respond to your initial approach, it is far better to be brave, take that first step and meet up quite quickly rather than to string them along in case someone better pops into your inbox.

This book has been written by a seasoned Internet dater. Over a period of ten years, Sarah Edwards had more than 80 Internet dates and in this book offers advice, help and tips to cover the good, the bad and the ugly faces of Internet dating.

From accepting being single to dealing with emotional baggage and issues, discovering the kind of relationship you want and personal safety to creating a brilliant online profile – this book will help guide you through the minefield of searching for love in cyberspace!

# Chapter One

# The Single Life . . . How Did You Get Here?

We become single for various reasons and chances are that if you ask a group of people why they are single they will all give a different account of the situations and circumstances of life that brought them to this point.

It is important to point out at this stage that there is *nothing* wrong with being single. Not having a partner or children or being part of a traditional nuclear family does not make you some kind of social outcast. Indeed many people prefer their own company to that of other people, some have careers that are so demanding that they simply would not support a relationship and others have just never found the 'right' person.

However, we are often extremely adept at convincing ourselves and others that we are really quite happy and content being single and that we fail to see the attraction of sharing our lives with anyone else. Seasoned singletons are masters of disguise and able to persuade just about anyone that we have accepted our lot in life and that being single is *far* better than being in a relationship for a myriad of reasons – some emotional, some physical and more often than not – some financial.

This book has been written to help anyone who is thinking of ditching the single life and is hoping to meet their soulmate, life partner or future spouse by trying their hand at Internet dating. It is worth noting here that as with all methods of meeting new people, Internet dating is not necessarily a one size fits all approach to hooking up with the love of your life.

However, it can be a lot of fun, makes for very interesting dates and, as I found myself, can really help you work out exactly what it is you want from a relationship, as well as those things that you really don't!

I was extremely surprised by the relationship that I finally found and Internet dating certainly showed me the right way and wrong way to try and attract Mr Right into my life. I hope that you enjoy your Internet dating journey as much as I did and that eventually you find exactly who you are looking for!

## More baggage than the lost luggage department at Heathrow?

Okay – we all have it. Whatever your age or situation there is a very real reason why we are single so the first step in developing your Internet dating career is to be very honest with yourself about why you are single and what baggage you are bringing with you.

Examining your 'baggage' is important because without doing this it is very easy for us to cover things up, hide from problems and ignore obvious reasons for our single status. Everyone expects their date to have had a bit of relationship 'previous'. It's inevitable – but it is *not* to be the main topic of conversation on the first date (or second, third or fourth!)

Looking at your own life and what has happened before is important to help you grow and learn as a person but it is not something that your latest prospect wants to know anything about – certainly not in the early days.

If you are going to put yourself out there in cyberspace and search for dates, companionship, love or your life partner, then acknowledging you are not perfect and you do have baggage is a crucial first step.

Maybe you have an ex-partner (or two or three?), some children, or you have been through a traumatic experience or illness that has left you feeling vulnerable and unsure of yourself. Perhaps you have suffered some financial setbacks, recovered from an addiction or been homeless or in prison. Whatever level of baggage you are carrying around with you, it might be worth considering some professional help or counselling to help you move through whatever it is that you have experienced. By sharing your baggage with someone else you will find that you can really move on and have a healthy approach to dating.

The last thing anyone should look for when Internet dating is someone to rescue them. This immediately makes you appear vulnerable and weak and you will not attract the kind of person who is right for you.

---

## Case study

John, 38, said: 'I was a classic relationship rebounder and went straight into a new relationship without taking a good look at the state my life was actually in. My new partner was very supportive and helped me sort out my financial problems and other issues, but once we had done that we realised that we didn't actually know each other very well. I had needed someone to rescue me and it was selfish. It was really a good few years before I could honestly say that all my baggage had finally been dealt with properly and I was ready to have a fully functioning and healthy relationship with someone. I decided to have a rest from online dating for a while and then went back to it when I had sorted myself out.'

---

Deal with that baggage first and it will stand you in good stead when you reach for your laptop and make your first excursion into looking for love online. It doesn't matter how long it takes for you to sort things out – all in good time.

# Time is a great healer

Recovering from a bad or unhealthy relationship takes time – just like anything else that impacts negatively on your life.

Jumping from one relationship to a search for another is inevitably a disaster, so give yourself a bit of time off before you start searching for love again. Take some time out to look after yourself and your children, if you have any, and do a bit of basic research about the kind of dating websites that are out there.

You may find that you just want to get back out there as soon as possible and forget about all the bad stuff that has happened. That is fine as long as you have really dealt with it all and can truly put it behind you.

Time does make things feel and look a lot better so if you are not super confident about writing your online profile and clicking that button to activate it – don't feel under any pressure to do so. Just because single friends have jumped straight in to the Internet dating arena and lined up a date every other night for the next three months, it doesn't mean that you have to do the same. We are all different and we all have different levels of confidence, tolerance and available time.

Internet dating can be all-consuming let alone time-consuming, so pace yourself! It's not a race to see how quickly you can meet someone. This is supposed to be fun and part of your single journey to learn more about yourself, so don't rush in and spoil it all.

## The parent trap – considering children

Not everyone who is single and reading this book will have children – it's not a pre requisite but it is a fact that we do have a lot of single parents in this country – in fact a quarter of all households are single-parent families. There is a lot of help available for single parents, from dating advice to benefits advice and this is covered in *Single Parents – The Essential Guide* Sarah Edwards, Need2Know.

Dating as a single parent is quite different to dating without having to consider children, and it is important to really think about what you are embarking on and how it is going to impact on your children.

Everyone has their own ideas of what works and what doesn't, but from my own experiences as a single parent of 11 years standing, I would advise that you keep your Internet dating career to yourself – at least at first.

We have all heard the delightful and heart-warming stories of children who are so desperate for their mum or dad to meet someone new that they sign up to Internet dating sites for them, and we have all seen *Sleepless in Seattle* a million times. However, real life has a nasty habit of biting us on the bum, so the sensible option is to keep things quiet and just get on with it without announcing it to your entire family.

Of course, if you have older children it is different and you can talk about relationships and dating in a grown up and constructive way. Younger children jump to conclusions quickly, and the last thing you want is for them to start getting fixated with a certain person, only to find that they really are not *the one*.

Apart from anything else – you are allowed to have a life that doesn't involve your children *all* the time and you are a grown-up. Go have your dates, just don't make a song and dance about it!

Try and organise your week so that you have at least one child-free evening for dates. This way you will literally have your date in the diary and you can build in time for getting ready and preparing for your evening without having to worry about cooking fish fingers and helping with homework for a change!

# Get it sorted . . . managing your own life before you even think about getting involved with someone else's

Are you amazing at solving everyone else's problems? Do friends come to you with their worries, woes and dilemmas? Single friends are brilliant at looking after other people and dealing with all their problems but often pretty rubbish at looking after themselves!

Can you put your hand on your heart and honestly say that you are really ready to begin Internet dating?

There will be plenty of people around you who are keen to both encourage and discourage your initial foray into Cupid's cyberspace, but ultimately you have to ask yourself if you are really ready for the next step.

Often it is very easy to distract ourselves from our own problems and difficulties by making radical changes and taking big steps to do new things. This can be a way of fooling ourselves that our lives are all hunky-dory, when in actual fact they are not. Dealing with other people's problems is admirable, kind and charitable, but if you are filling your life with someone else's issues and not even beginning to look carefully at your own, then there is probably something not quite right and you may need to spend a bit of time working on yourself first!

This is, of course, quite scary and you may feel the need to seek some professional help in the form of counselling or therapy first. A list of useful contacts can be found in the back of this book for anyone who feels they would benefit from this kind of help.

There really is no point in trying to fool yourself into moving on if you know that things in your own life need sorting out first. By doing this you are not only kidding yourself but also anyone who you date. You will not feel comfortable, confident or relaxed in someone else's company if you don't have a clue about what is happening in your own life.

Another major consideration is that people are not really keen to hear about all your troubles and problems on your first date. There is nothing quite as unattractive as someone who is needy, bitter, resentful or self-obsessed. Although getting out and meeting people is really important, your frame of mind is crucial to a successful date. If you approach it negatively, chances are it won't go well. However, with a positive but realistic outlook you will be in for an enjoyable and interesting time. For more help with staying positive check out Sue Stone's book *Live, Laugh, Love* (see the book list). It is fantastic and will really help you put a positive spin on even the darkest situations.

It's fair to say that you may not meet the person of your dreams immediately, but try to treat each date as just that – a date. Not a proposal of marriage or even an option for a second date – just a date. Everyone you meet will bring a small, new dimension to your life so don't write a date off as a disaster just because you didn't 'click'. Who knows, they may have a friend or a relation who might just be perfect for you, so keep an open mind.

Spend some time looking after yourself and sorting out your own issues before you even start asking anyone else about theirs. It may sound selfish but trust me – it's the way forward!

# Summing Up

* Your first forays into Internet dating are really useful for helping to improve your self-confidence, and should be treated as a small stepping stone along your journey.

* Try not to get carried away with the idea that you are about to meet 'the one' and instead take a positive experience from every date you have.

* It is very easy to come away from a date feeling disappointed and let down if there is no mention of doing it again. However, remember that the people you meet are transient in your life and try hard not to let their reaction and response to you to impact negatively on how you feel about yourself.

# Chapter Two

# Are You Ready?

When a relationship ends, particularly if you are the injured party, it is a natural reaction for some of us to make every effort to get out there and start dating – if only to prove to our previous partners that we are still desirable. Of course, the reality is that we don't need to prove anything to anyone apart from ourselves, but in those early days of single life our emotions are often very erratic and our common sense is quickly forgotten! We tend to think that just because our previous partners no longer wanted us, there is bound to be someone else who will. This may well be true – but easy does it!

This book was written as a guide for anyone who is considering Internet dating, however before you even consider surfing the Web for a suitable site to use, it is really important to think about yourself, how you are feeling and if you are truly ready to start seeking out love in cyberspace.

Having the confidence to find a website, build a profile and start contacting potential dates is a big step, and although it is a lot of fun, you do need to be completely sure that you are prepared emotionally for this new phase in your life. Once your profile is out there and the contact between you and your new dates begins, it is often difficult to handle and many Internet daters find that it is too much too soon. It is easy to forget that essentially you are telling millions of complete strangers a lot of detailed information about you. At the beginning of your Internet dating journey you may have a surge of supreme confidence and just think 'to hell with it – what have I got to lose?'. The fact of the matter is that it may take you some time before you meet your prince or princess charming, and along the way there are bound to be a few potholes and bumps in the road.

Being prepared and ready to get out there and meet new people is more important than actually meeting them. This may sound strange, but unless you are happy, confident and secure with who you are, you will inevitably attract the wrong kind of person. When relationships end, our self-confidence and self-esteem can be at an all-time low. Consequently, you may well be needy and requiring emotional support. That is not what dating is about. Dating is about widening your social circle, experiencing the chance to meet new people and make new friends and developing your confidence in social situations. If you go out there looking for a counsellor or therapist or someone to moan to about your dreadful life and the appalling way your last partner treated you – you will end up spending your precious spare time with people who will not be a good and positive influence in your life.

## Issues – we all have them

While they may not all be massive, difficult or even life-changing, we all have issues in our lives that need to be managed effectively. This is an essential part of moving on and when we acknowledge our past, what has happened and why, we are able to then make plans for our future. It may be painful and upsetting as we try and tackle these problems and situations, but it is a good investment in your future self!

Friends are often a great source of support, and I fully acknowledge that when it came to my status as a singleton, my friends were supportive in all kinds of ways. Being able to talk about things that are bothering you is important – the alternative is to bottle everything up and keep it to yourself. This might seem like the easiest option at the outset, but further down the line the issues that you have not yet dealt with may well come back to haunt you and could cause problems for your new relationship or dating career.

So what kind of issues can hold you back? The list is almost endless because issues are so personal and there is no 'one size fits all' solution to things that have happened in our lives and continue to affect our abilities to have relationships and move forward.

For example, perhaps you suffer from poor confidence levels and low self-esteem because you have issues around how you look or your achievements in your life? This could be because you were rejected and replaced by a former partner who you consider left you for someone who was more attractive/cleverer/richer.

Perhaps you have concerns about being abandoned or left alone again and this is hampering your attempts at having a healthy attitude towards dating and meeting new people?

Perhaps you have health concerns and feel uncomfortable discussing this with new people you meet online?

Whatever your issues may be there are ways of dealing with them that will be effective at helping you to move forward with your life, embrace being single *and* have fun looking for love online!

# Moving forward – early steps

So you have made the decision to look at the prospects that Internet dating offers you as a single person, but are you happy being single? This may be a rather ridiculous statement to make in a book that has been written to help you find love online, but the harsh truth is that unless you like yourself, are kind to yourself and accept that right *now* you are *single* – you may get off to a shaky start.

Have you really and truly experienced life as a single person, or have you spent the last few months or years being constantly on the hunt for a partner? Have you relied endlessly on the goodwill of friends and family to prop you up? Have you expected everyone to listen to you endlessly going on and on about how rubbish being single is and how all you need is a new man/woman in your life and then everything will be perfect?

Or . . . have you positively embraced being single by enjoying the independence and seeking out new and exciting experiences to share with people? Have you worked on yourself to improve your self-esteem? Have you accepted that you are single and that actually life is good?

Before you embark on a stint of Internet dating, it is *crucial* that you have acknowledged positively all that single life can offer you. From my own experiences, I know that once I stopped being needy, desperate and dull about being the perennial 'Bridget Jones' at dinner parties – life got a whole lot better!

My career started to improve, I lost weight and started meeting some fabulous new people who were interested in the stories that I had to share about the positive spin I had put on single life. This all happened because I started to turn my negative thoughts about being single into positive ones. It didn't happen overnight, but trust me – it's the way forward!

It became pretty obvious to me that it was unlikely that I would attract any new men into my life if I continued to spend all my time at my kitchen table, moaning about the size of my thighs!

By taking small steps to look at life a little differently, you will reap big rewards in the coming months.

## Feeling good?

Feeling good and looking good go pretty much hand in hand. If you are enjoying life and getting out and about experiencing new things with different people then, by default, you will feel and appear more attractive to potential dates.

If you are hiding away and permanently glued to the television or computer screen, what will you possibly have to talk about when you *do* go on some dates? It is true that life is what we make it, and to get the most out of life we sometimes have to step outside our comfort zones and do some quite radical things!

If you don't feel great about yourself there are many ways that you can turn this around. If, like me, your weight has long been an issue then there is help out there for everyone. From your best friend to your sister, your GP or your local slimming club, there will be a method that suits you and your lifestyle that will help you get the body you want. It's important to mention at this point that losing weight, getting fitter or changing your hair colour is all about *you*. You should not be doing these things to please anyone else. However, if losing a little weight, toning up and having a bit of a makeover makes *you* feel good – then that is the way forward. (If you feel you would like some help getting your weight under control, take a look at *Forget the Fear of Food* by Chris Fenn, Need2Know.)

If there are other areas of your life that need a little attention and you feel will boost your confidence when you start looking for love online, then now is a great time to tackle them as well. One subject that I get asked about again and again concerns parents. Often single parents feel that because they have devoted many years to bringing up their children, they no longer have anything of any value to bring to a date. They worry that they have become boring and will not have anything in common with anyone else.

This is simply not true! Firstly, there are dating websites that have been set up specifically for single parents and secondly, parenting is one big exciting journey that's often stressful but it equips you for all sorts of exciting possibilities! If you haven't worked for a while and you are worried that you have become dull then think again! If you have reached a point in your life where you do have some extra time on your hands then consider taking a short college course or joining a group of some sort. Learning something new and meeting new people will really help when you get out there and start Internet dating.

# Meeting new people

Do you panic at the thought of meeting new people? Is that why you think Internet dating is the way forward . . . because chances are you can chat online and never actually *meet* anyone in the flesh?

Well if that is the case you need to have a rethink . . . and fast! People who sign up to dating websites are handing over their hard-earned cash and spending time creating a killer profile in the hope that they will actually meet a *real* person. Hiding behind your profile and making excuses not to meet up with people can only last for so long before your matches make their excuses and start looking elsewhere.

Instead of worrying about meeting new people, accept that this is all part of the dating process and that if you don't get on you never have to see them again, but if you don't try . . . you'll never know! If meeting strangers does put the fear of God into you then ask some friends to invite you to a few get-togethers first, or consider joining a group locally so that you can meet people on a casual basis.

# Managing your expectations

This is all very tricky! I used to tell massive big fibs about how I felt about Internet dating and they went something like this: 'Oh I don't care if he doesn't like me . . . plenty more fish in the sea . . . it's just a date . . . got to go through the motions . . . I don't want a *proper* relationship anyway . . . I am quite happy being single . . .' and so on.

The reality was that in time, I *was* very happy being single and this ultimately helped me have a loving and committed relationship, but during the height of my Internet dating career, I hoped that every date I went on would be *the one*. Date after date after date left me deflated, with my self-confidence plummeting to the ground and my self-esteem in tatters. I got to the point where I wondered how much longer I could go on picking myself up, dusting myself off – and starting again.

It is vital that you are honest about what you hope and expect to gain from Internet dating because this will shape the kind of dates that you have. For example, one Internet dater I spoke to made it quite clear that he was only interested in a 'relationship' based purely on sex and nights at expensive hotels. He claimed not to care about falling in love or having any long-term commitment. He only attracted women into his life who wanted that kind of arrangement. I am sure you don't need me to tell you that this kind of lifestyle rarely leads to long-term happiness or fulfilment and his foray into 'friends with benefits' was pretty short-lived when he realised his date was actually enjoying the same kind of arrangement with quite a few wealthy men! A few years on and he is now happily living with a fabulous woman who adores him – domestic bliss! This all happened when he started being honest about what he really wanted instead of saying what he *thought* potential partners wanted to hear.

So – be clear about what you want and honest with the people you meet. This does not mean that if you one day you hope to marry and have children that you should say this on a first date! However, you can make it clear that you are looking for a proper relationship and someone to share your life with.

**Need2Know**

# Summing Up

- As a basic rule, try and treat each date as just that – one date. Who knows what might happen?

- Be honest with yourself and accept that it may take some time to meet someone who you truly click with.

- Be honest and clear with yourself and the people you meet from the outset – that way everyone knows where they stand.

# Chapter Three

# Would Like to Meet . . .

In the course of our daily lives we meet people. Whether it is bumping into friends at the school gate while dropping the kids off at school, meeting up in the community as we go about our daily errands, or making new contacts through work or study, as a general rule we will have contact with people for a large part of our week.

However, touching base and catching up with people we are familiar with is one thing – meeting new people whom we know nothing about – is quite another!

As a single person in an ideal world you would be introduced to potential dates by friends, family or work colleagues. Maybe a friend of a friend or a brother or sister of a friend. The reality is this doesn't work for everyone and that is why the Internet dating business is clearly booming! The people we surround ourselves with in our daily lives are people who have an empathy with us, who know us, understand us and have shared interests or opinions. We feel comfortable with them and enjoy their company and most importantly – we trust them. Trust has to be gained over time and takes investment on the part of both friends in order for a relationship to flourish.

When we meet new colleagues at work, or fellow students at college or university there is already come common ground, when we meet strangers from the Internet, no matter what they *may* have told you in an email or on the phone, it is possible that you won't necessarily have any immediate common ground – apart from the fact that you are both searching for love online.

Now is the time to really think carefully about the kind of person you would like to meet and the qualities that are important to you. Single people who I have spoken to during the research phase of this book have given me mixed responses to the question about the kind of person they are looking for. Some were adamant that good looks, success and lots of money were not that important, while for others – those were *the* most important factors.

We are all different and want different things from life, work and our relationships, and meeting new people is exciting and interesting. However, if you are not clear with yourself about the kind of new people you would like to attract into your life, you may find that your dates are hard work and more of a chore than a pleasure!

## What or who are you looking for and why?

Important questions that you ask yourself before you meet your first date, will really help you clarify *why* you have decided to try Internet dating and *who* you would like to meet.

If you have been single for some time, you may find it very difficult to really be honest with yourself and others about the kind of new people you would like to meet. When my husband left me I was 30 and had been with him since I was a teenager! Trust me – being thrust out onto the singles' market having had only one other significant relationship during my entire life made for some very tricky early dates! I had no idea who or what I was looking for and actually ended up in some very unsavoury situations with men because I thought they were the kind of people I *should* be meeting. Instead of listening to myself and being honest about the kind of man I did want to eventually meet, I was too busy listening to other people tell me what I should and shouldn't be doing. I had one friend telling me to only go out with someone who would support me financially (even though I didn't *need* anyone else's money!) and another warning me to avoid anyone with children or who was more than two years older than me! I am so glad I stopped listening to them because the man I ended up with is eight years older than me, has four children and is certainly not a millionaire!

So take some time to think about your life and the things you enjoy doing and are interested in. What kind of person are you? You will find that whatever Internet dating site you decide to choose will offer you the chance to write a profile of yourself so that your potential dates can find out about your likes and dislikes. Think about this carefully and make sure you are brutally honest! There is more information about creating your online profile later in the book, but for now just make a simple list of what you *do* want and what you definitely do *not* want!

# Being clear about why you are Internet dating

Internet dating has been harshly criticised by many people because it is often seen as a playground for disingenuine people who have scant regard for the feelings of others. In every walk of life and every dating option you will encounter people who are not looking for the same thing as you, and that is why it is vital that you are clear about why you have chosen to look for love in this way.

Internet dating is often seen as the last resort, and something that desperate singletons do who can't meet people in a 'normal' way. This is not the case at all, and there are very valid reasons to consider Internet dating as the way to meet new people and maybe find love.

For many of us, joining a traditional introduction or dating agency just isn't an option. Apart from the fact that most of them have now been replaced by online dating sites, an agency approach does not suit everyone's lifestyle. Personal ads in newspapers or magazines are fraught with potential problems and offer you just a very small pool of potential dates. The Internet however is massive and growing all the time and you will never run out of new sites to try or people to match with. The Internet is also ideal for people with busy lives or for those who work shifts or work away a lot. It offers you access to thousands and thousands of dating sites and I guarantee that there is one out there for everyone – whatever you are looking for! Internet dating is quick, simple and if you have had enough you can hide your profile or cancel your membership. Don't enter into Internet dating as a last resort – be positive and optimistic and embrace the new opportunities that the World Wide Web of love may have to offer!

# Peer pressure

These days, Internet dating is a perfectly socially acceptable way to meet new people and look for companionship, friendship and relationships. You will always hear horror stories from people who had dates from hell – I should know because, after all, I did have 80 Internet dates and most of them were pretty challenging!

However, it did not stop me from picking myself up, dusting myself down and doing it all over again – despite protestations to the contrary from my friends! In fact, as time went on I discovered that the very friends who had been dismissive of Internet dating at the beginning had actually started to have a go themselves!

The best way to deal with any kind of pressure from friends or family is to not make a big deal of it. I chose not to tell anyone about my dates apart from one close friend, because I got increasingly tired of people asking me how things had gone and then making trite comments when I told them it hadn't been great.

Remember that this new chapter in your life is about *you* – and Internet dating is what *you* want to try. You may find the love of your life or you may not, but ultimately it is nobody else's business and, after all, it is you who has to live with the consequences of your actions. As long as you are honest with yourself and treat yourself and your dates kindly – how many dates you have and with whom can be kept to yourself.

## Keeping things quiet

If you have a good friend who you can truly trust and you want to disclose your dating activity to them then I recommend that you do. There are two very good reasons for telling someone what you are up to, and the first concerns personal safety. Later in the book we will talk more about your first dates and how and where to meet, but telling someone that you are going out to meet a new person who you have never met before is a good idea. That way, someone knows where you are and if you don't come back at the allotted time they can raise the alarm if necessary.

Another good reason for sharing your dating news is to illicit some feedback. Being single can be tremendous and I had many years of being happily single and having lots of fun. However, I really needed to share my dating experiences with someone if only to make me feel better when things didn't quite go according to plan! It was also great to get tips and advice from someone who had been such a prolific dater back in the day!

I learned a great deal from my experiences of meeting people and communicating with people online, and although at times I found it hard I am glad that I continued to make the effort. However, after a while I realised that there was little point in telling everyone everything that was going on. I started to feel under considerable pressure to have a 'good' date and life just isn't like that. Most of my dates in the early days were disappointing and I found that if I had to dissect every experience with everyone I knew I would never be able to move on and feel confident about myself and the way I behaved when I met new people. I often found that rather than give my confidence a much needed boost, I was actually starting to react negatively to what had happened because I was simply over analysing. It is very worthwhile to unravel challenging experiences because that is how we learn – just don't over share and remember that you won't get on with everyone – such is the nature of the human condition.

# Be honest

Honesty is the best policy – particularly in the Internet dating arena. Obviously the Internet does a great job of insulating us from real life to a large extent, and it is true that we can be anyone we want to be online. However, I can honestly say that every profile I created was accurate and honest and it stood me in good stead. Don't do crazy things like say you are into clubbing or skiing or bungee jumping if you are more of a book at bedtime and a stroll round the park kind of person. Pretending to be more adventurous than we are is a common mistake made by Internet daters because for some reason we think we are just not exciting enough as we are. The reality is that if you lie and say you like things that you clearly have no interest in or even experience of, you will come unstuck soon enough.

# Summing Up

- Be you and be honest and you will encounter people who appreciate you for who you are – not what you think you should be.

- Try not to let friends and family influence you or tell you what to do.

- We meet potential partners in a variety of different ways now, and Internet dating is a great way to extend your social circle, improve your own interpersonal skills and increase your self-confidence – it's also a lot of fun and that seems to be one thing that well-meaning friends can easily forget!

# Chapter Four

# Why Internet Dating?

Why bother with the Internet to try and find love? After all won't we just inevitably bump into the love of our life in the queue at the supermarket? Won't our eyes meet across a crowded room? Or maybe our best friend will finally realise that we *are* in fact the love of their life? Mmmmm . . . and maybe we might just win the lottery next week too!

The trouble is that although all of the above are perfectly valid and tried and tested ways of finding love – and there are plenty of movie scripts that are borne out of all of those scenarios – real life doesn't always happen quite like that.

When I was single and really struggling with the way my life had turned out, a good friend asked me how I thought I was ever going to find anyone to go out with if I spent all day sat at my kitchen table? It was a good point, and although I probably didn't react very positively at the time – he was right! There comes a time in our lives when those romantic mishaps just don't happen – and it's not something that you can force or plan in any way. Either you will just bump into your life partner or you won't – but instead of sitting there and watching endless episodes of *Sex and the City* in the hope that your Mr (or Miss) Big will walk into your life – get out there and start living a little!

Everyone in your life will have an opinion on your foray into finding love online – the best advice I can give you is to research the whole process so that *you* are happy with your decision. Remember – this new chapter in your life is about you – not your friends and family who are probably already part of a couple and have long forgotten about what the single life is all about!

# Pros

The way that we meet people has changed immeasurably over the last few years, and we are now firmly in an age where the Internet is seen as the accepted, obvious and almost essential tool when it comes to managing many aspects of our lives. Of course meeting people through cyberspace does not suit everyone, but if you haven't yet tried it – read on!

We apply for jobs and finance online, we shop online, research products, send emails instead of letters and greetings cards, and even look forward to our daily horoscope and news bulletins pinging into our inboxes. We also work and study online, chat to friends on Skype and rely heavily on our Internet connections for our smart phone, iPads and laptops to make sure we keep in touch with the rest of the world.

We are in an age of information overload, and the communication superhighway that is the Internet is an obvious, modern and relatively natural progression when it comes to dating and meeting new people.

Using the Internet to attract new people into our lives is both convenient and fun. We can surf and research to find the right site for us, read articles and information about the experiences that other people have had on dating websites and ultimately make a choice of dating site and upload and update our profile. Checking messages is easy as most sites alert you via email to let you know that someone has been in touch, and it's also easy and quick to review any new matches or members who might be a potential date.

The sheer volume of sites available makes the Internet an obvious choice for anyone who is keen to meet as many people as possible, and with new sites launching all the time you will find the right one for you. For people who have difficulty with mobility or face other challenges, the Internet can be life-changing and put them in touch with people who are in the same position as them. This opens up a world of possibility for anyone who faces physical or emotional challenges that can often create feelings of isolation and exclusion.

By being able to read about people and see photos of potential dates, we are automatically in a stronger position than if we were to go on a series of blind dates, as we have a heads-up before we meet new people. Knowing a little bit about someone before you meet them means that you have some idea of their interests, hobbies and work. This basic information can form the beginnings of some great, insightful conversations and having access to details such as what somebody does for a living also means that if there is an awkward silence you can always fill it with a relevant question!

If you decide that Internet dating is not for you, your profile can be instantly removed and your membership cancelled.

A growing number of people find their partners through Internet dating sites, and therefore there is a ready-made database of people who are happy to share their experiences and knowledge with you. Since its early days, Internet dating has developed into a sophisticated and relatively well-moderated platform for introducing yourself to new people, and it is getting better all the time.

# Cons

There will always be people who are adamant that the Internet is *not* the way to meet new people, because it is dangerous and full of profiles of people who lie, embellish and try to trick people into meeting them. There are plenty of horror stories of Internet dates that have gone wrong and turned into terrifying situations. These are not to be overlooked, but it is worth remembering that dangerous people existed long before the Internet came along, and as long as you are sensible, safe and follow the rules of dating (see later chapters for advice and tips) it can be fun and enjoyable.

However, you do need to exercise some caution and a *lot* of common sense. Remember that you can pretty much be anyone you want to be on the Internet, so it is important to have both an open mind and take care of yourself – both online and when you finally decide to meet up with someone. Internet dating has a big emphasis on balance and making sure that while you do give yourself the chance to embrace new opportunities, you make sure that you are comfortable at all times with the decisions you are making.

You should never feel pressured into meeting someone, and if you start to feel anxious, nervous or uncomfortable about anything then it is probably time to have a rethink.

Possibly one of the biggest cons of Internet dating is the fact that once you have started to communicate online, it can be difficult and awkward when you change your mind, meet someone else, or simply have a change in your circumstances that means you need a break from it for a while. Decent, honest people who are genuinely looking for dates, a partner, romance or a relationship should understand your reasons for breaking off contact – either temporarily or permanently, and should respect your wish to be left alone. If you find that you are being 'stalked' or pestered by someone then sometimes the only option is to delete your profile. If you have exchanged email addresses then you will have to go through the process of blocking them. If the problem becomes really serious then it is worth contacting the dating site direct and registering a complaint with them. Sites will only improve if we tell them when things go wrong.

## Success stories . . . and horror stories

Unfortunately, there are always plenty of people who delight in the horror stories that Internet dating creates. It would be naive of me, and irresponsible, not to mention that sometimes the world of cyber love does not go according to plan. However, during the course of researching this book, and interviewing countless couples over the years for various articles on Internet dating, it is clear that some relationships definitely do stand the test of time.

A salient point to emphasise here is the fact that no matter how we meet our partner – it may or may not work out according to plan. Therefore there is no reason to suspect that just because Cupid worked his magic over the Internet, our future relationships are any more – or less – secure.

Horror stories about Internet dating continue to abound, and more often than not these are the tales that make the headlines – as opposed to the stories of love blossoming and resulting in marriage, babies and a happy ever after.

With our lives being the way they are and pressure on time being ever increasing, many Internet daters would argue that they simply do not have the time to go on endless blind dates in the hope that they will eventually meet someone. Of course, with Internet dating, as with any other form of dating, there are expectations. One of those expectations will be that people will expect to meet each other in person eventually. Of course, with the power of the Internet there is the option to effectively 'weed out' any people who do not quite meet your requirements, before having to meet them for real.

There are, of course, no true 100% guarantees that no matter how careful you have been during the vetting procedure, that the person you do choose to meet is as delightful, funny, attractive and easy-going as you may have been led to believe from their profile!

And this is where many of the horror stories begin! I actually found that in many cases the men I decided to meet up with were a far cry from their photos and many lied about their ages as well (and I always thought it was just women who did that!) I was always honest, uploaded recent photos and had no need to lie about my age, and yet often it was the disingenuine men who decided not to ask *me* out for second date!

On a very serious note, there are people who actively use Internet dating sites to commit fraud, deception and other crimes. At the end of 2011, the Serious Organised Crime Agency started to investigate the UK's online dating industry following research that suggested up to 200,000 people had been tricked by overseas conmen who offered love online but used the contact to persuade matches to give them large amounts of money.

In one high profile case that was still under investigation as this book went to print, a man was accused of tricking at least five British women into handing over £750,000 after replying to ads on dating websites. Unfortunately, online dating scams have become one of the most lucrative methods for conmen and conwomen to defraud Britons. With at least 1,400 dating websites operating in this country alone, it is easy to see why fraudsters use them as their target.

The advice from websites is to always communicate through their site and build relationships up over time, rather than give out personal details, and never, ever give any money to anyone for any reason.

## Proceed with caution

So with all these cautionary tales I expect you are wondering why on earth I should be writing a book to help guide you through the love jungle of Internet dating! The reason is simple. It can be a lot of fun and you will undoubtedly meet some new and interesting people. You may decide never to see them again – but that is *your* decision and unless you get out there and start searching for the love of your life you may never know.

When we try anything new in our lives it takes us a while to get used to it. Whether it's a new job, a new fitness regime, a new hobby or even taking the plunge to get a new hairstyle, it all takes time to adjust, and trying Internet dating is no different. I have spoken to people who went on three dates and on the fourth found the love of their life. I have spoken to people who ended up in long-term relationships with the brother, sister or friend of one of their Internet dates, and I have also interviewed countless people who having tried and tried to get it right in cyberspace and after numerous dates finally met the right person to share their life with. A good friend once said to me that you have to kiss a lot of frogs . . . and how right she was!

So, instead of setting off on this new adventure having already written the script – take time to adjust to this new interest and treat it as something that will enhance your life in one way or another – rather than something that will change it forever. Nobody knows how things are going to turn out when we start something new.

If you proceed with caution and don't let Internet dating take over your life, it will be fun and you will notice some really positive changes in yourself. However, if it becomes an unhealthy and unnatural obsession that starts to change your behaviour in a negative way – it is time to take a step back and reign things in a little. Try to see this time in your life as one of really positive personal growth that could lead to . . . well . . . who knows what! It's exciting and you have already made the decision to do it so make the most of it, give it your very best shot and see what happens. It's not for everyone – but it could well be for you!

# Summing Up

- Friends and family are always quick to judge and give their opinion about our single statuses, and it is difficult not to start believing the hype sometimes! We know that they have our best interests at heart, but in many cases the people who give you the advice (solicited or not!) are often in long-term relationships – or what I call 'the smugly marrieds' of the world! They may mean well but unless they have tried Internet dating themselves they are simply not in a position to tell you what to do. Yes they may well have read endless stories in the tabloid press about some terrible things that have happened to people who use the Internet to find love, but by contrast they won't have picked up on any of the positive stories.

- Take time to read some testimonials on some of the dating websites – in some cases you will be able to contact the people concerned through the website.

- Many thousands of people have found love online, with a careful and measured approach to this new way of meeting people, there is no reason why you can't too.

# Chapter Five

# How it Works

Well if you have read this far – *congratulations*! I am delighted that you are still seriously thinking of taking a plunge into the world of Internet dating. So how does it all work then?

In this chapter we will look at staying safe, how matching processes work, choosing a site that suits you and making sure that Internet dating doesn't take over your life.

Sites use all manner of software to 'scientifically' match you with potential partners. The way you build your profile will determine how you are matched up and who you are matched with, so it is important to be clear and honest when you submit your details. Most sites allow profile updates to be made so if you make a mistake you can always log in and make corrections, amendments or additions.

## Safety first – personal safety

If you just bumped into someone in the street and your eyes met and then something was muttered about having a coffee or a drink sometime and then you exchanged phone numbers, chances are that when you regaled your friends with this tale – they wouldn't be too alarmed. In fact they would probably tell you to go for it and enjoy yourself.

However, how would the same friends react to the news that you had met someone online, had exchanged a few emails and were planning to meet for a drink? With option 1 you know nothing about each other – you have literally just bumped into each other. There is no previous contact, no profile matching – it's a chance liaison.

With the online option, some kind of background has already been established. You have probably met online because your profiles suited each other and you wanted the same thing, shared the same interests and so on.

Before you start screaming and throw this book at the nearest wall, I know that we can be anyone we like on the Internet. But we can also be anyone we like and say whatever we like in real life too. The point here is this – personal safety is important no matter how you are meeting people.

There are some basic common sense rules that I recommend you learn, memorise and recite to yourself before each date to avoid the possibility of putting yourself in any kind of personal danger and these are all explained in chapter 9. When it comes to safety online – before that all-important first date – there are also some tips to consider to ensure you stay safe online.

- When you build your profile be honest and clear about who you would like to meet. There is more information later in the book on how to write a winning profile, but as a starting point – do not drop in any personal information or photographs that could make things uncomfortable for you.

- Most dating sites have a strict code of conduct but not all, so be aware of this when you join and spend some time looking at other profiles first to see how much or little information they offer. If you don't feel comfortable revealing as much as other users are, then move on and try a different site.

- Take things slowly and no matter how fabulous your first matches are or how flattered you feel by the attention you may get, don't be too quick to give out your personal contact details. All websites give you the option to continue contact through their secure systems and it is a good idea to do this early on.

- If the attention you receive is not quite what you hoped for and you feel uncomfortable and awkward about the type of messages you are receiving, then block the person who is contacting you. Sometimes, even when it is blindingly obvious to you that what you have is certainly not a match made in heaven – or cyberspace – the other party may just find that difficult to accept. The easiest way to deal with this is to block them – and that is why it is crucial not to give out your details until you are confident that you will want to meet up.

- If the worst happens and you do find yourself being bothered by someone who you would rather not be in touch with any more, contact your email and mobile phone provider for information and advice about how to block people from contacting you.

# Matching processes – the science behind cyber love

So is there really much science involved when it comes to matching single people searching for love? Basically you fill in your details and you indicate the kind of person you would like to meet, their age, eye colour, even their body shape and their interests, occupation and believe it or not . . . their salary! Then the matching process begins and hooks up like-minded people with the hope that they will get along just fine and have a long, happy life together forever after!

Of course, the reality is that despite your personal preferences you may be excluding some potential matches for the very reason that you are being a little too specific. I call this the 'tick box syndrome' and I have seen many, many single girlfriends adopt this approach to their dating careers. For various reasons, often based on previous bad experiences with men, they decide that what they want is someone with loads of money aged up to 45 (but no older), who is a successful businessman, with children who are independent (in other words – grown up and off their hands) who is available for fancy nights out and weekends at top European destinations. Some of my girlfriends hit the jackpot – they got exactly what they wanted – or what they *thought* they wanted – or thought they *should* have for whatever reason. Some of this comes down to acceptance by their social circle, some of it comes down to the fact that they truly want a financial lifeboat to rescue them and float off to some far-flung life of luxury. But the thought of dating a plumber with an average income who is kind and funny with a couple of children who are still at school would horrify them – even though in some cases they have ended up in the lap of luxury, but seriously unhappy with life.

The point here is to be realistic about your matching criteria, after all, few of the girlfriends I mentioned above had the same financial or domestic status as the men they were trying to meet. Consequently, they had little in common with each other. Be flexible and if you make small compromises to widen your search and meet more interesting people you may find that the person you end up with is not who you were looking for at all, but is just perfect for you.

And after all, your future relationship is up to you – it's not about dating people just because of what your friends think of them, or because you have to compete with them. It's about being happy with someone who you trust and want to build some memories with. And remember, meeting online may well be the start of something wonderful, but it's what happens offline that will determine how your relationship really works out.

## Shop around

Currently, the Internet dating market is worth an estimated £2.5 billion (2012). This means that not only is there plenty of money to be made and loads of single people to choose from, but it also means there are plenty of websites to surf!

The amount of single parents in the UK is set to hit the two million mark over the next year or so – and they make up a large percentage of the singles' market in this country. For single parents looking for love, the Internet is ideal because it is so easy and convenient. You can surf the Net once the children are at school or in bed, and take your time to check out any potential matches. There are plenty of dating sites just for single parents and a quick search on Google reveals 1.3 million hits for a variety of sites to suit all parents – whatever their situation.

There are plenty of mainstream dating sites, but if you have a particular penchant for people in uniform, those who sail boats or play golf, or if you are seeking dates with professional people – the world is your oyster as well because niche dating sites are growing in popularity all the time. It is clear that as a nation of Internet daters we are pretty picky about the kind of people we would like to meet and the Internet dating industry is certainly doing a good job of stepping up to the mark to give us plenty of choice.

## Obligations Vs obsessions

So what happens when you have finally done your market research, decided on a site and started searching for love? Later in the book we will look at online etiquette, but initially it is very easy to get very carried away with what you are doing. The line between obligation and obsession can be a very narrow one, and it is tempting to let your new Internet dating hobby take over your life. There are certain rules that you will need to consider once you have been hooked up with some matches, and while it is only polite and courteous to respond and reply to any messages that you receive, to constantly be logging in to your new Internet dating site account and checking for messages will take over your life unless you put some strict boundaries in place.

Don't let your quest for online love become an antisocial obsession! In order for you to get the most from your Internet dating experience it is true that you need to invest some time in creating a good profile and making the first move with some of your matches. However, this new dimension to your social life should be an enhancement, not a chore and should complement the rest of your life rather than dominate it.

Set aside some time every day to check your inbox, review new matches and tweak your profile. Make it clear to anyone who you are in contact with that you only log in once or twice a day and that they shouldn't be concerned if you don't get back to them immediately. If you establish some rules at the beginning it will help you and any new friends you meet along the way.

## Can money buy you love?

In all honesty – of course it can't! However, a small investment in a good dating website could mean you meet some new and interesting people, and who knows – maybe get a bit of practice at dating again. Of course there are plenty of free dating websites available and using these initially is a good way to dip your toe into the pool of Internet dating and see if you like it before you take the plunge and hand over your hard-earned cash.

Keeping a clear head and a sense of perspective is really important, and you must be prepared to manage your expectations – no matter how many encouraging testimonials you might find on a dating website from happy and loved-up customers. Remember that dating websites are big businesses and the owners of the sites will only ever publicise the good results they get. Just because you pay a hefty fee to join a site does not guarantee that you will find the love of your life, so start slowly, do your homework and exercise some common sense before you blow your life savings!

# Summing Up

- There are new dating sites popping up every day, and this can be both good and bad, as too much choice can almost be overwhelming.

- It is worth spending some time thinking about the kind of person you want to meet and what the most important things on your list are for a potential relationship. This way you can decide if you think a niche or specialist dating site would be a better option than a general Internet dating site.

- Researching your options and thinking carefully about what it is you really want from your Internet dating experience will inevitably help you to focus your attention in the right areas, and save you valuable time in your search for cyber love.

# Chapter Six

# The Right Site

In the last chapter we touched briefly on the enormous amount and variety of Internet dating websites that are available. This is generally speaking a good thing – as long as you are clear about the kind of person you want to meet and the relationship you hope to have as a result.

So what *is* the right site for you? Below are some questions that might help you decide on the kind of person you want to meet, and the type of website that is right for you. There are no right or wrong answers – your answers will provide you with some basic foundations and a starting point for some Internet dating activity. Make a note of all your answers, as this will help you to build a plan about the kind of dating you hope to do and the sort of people you would like to meet.

## What do you *really* want?

- Are you prepared to invest money to subscribe to a paid for Internet dating site?

- How much are you prepared to pay each month?

- Are you interested in meeting someone with the same interests as you or someone who might introduce you to some new life experiences?

- How important is it to you that your potential date is very good-looking, a certain age, has a particular hair colour or skin colour or ethnicity?

- How important to you are religious and cultural beliefs, commitments and traditions?

- Are you accepting of other people's situations and commitments?

- Do you want to meet someone who has children or who would like children in the future?

- Do you want a full-time, committed relationship with exclusivity?

- Do you want a relationship that is part-time, based on occasional dates, that is mutually beneficial but without any proper, formal commitment?

- Do you want a relationship with someone who has a specific job, earning potential or lifestyle?

- Do you eventually hope to get married and have a family?

- Are you more interested in meeting someone from another country?

- Does a relationship based purely on online contact appeal to you more?

- Do you have time to spend building a good, honest, solid profile on your chosen Internet dating site and regularly answer any contact messages that you receive?

- Are you confident and comfortable using the Internet, and understand that if you do join an Internet dating site you will be expected to upload a photograph of yourself and write a profile that will provide other users with information about you?

## We are *not* all the same

You may have friends who have either used dating websites in the past or are using one or more now. They may be a very good source of research and opinion about the Internet dating scene and will no doubt be on hand to offer tips and advice about what to do and what not to do. We do, of course, trust our friends and value their opinion greatly – particularly when it comes to our relationships, or potential relationships.

However, no matter how much we do love and trust our friends and how much value we place on their opinions and comments, it is really important to remember that we are all different, and that is why our friends are important – they often provide us with a new and different take on life that makes us see things in a different way.

## Case study

Amy, 30, met her boyfriend, Matt, 39, on a dating site that specifically links up professional people. Amy said: 'I had tried blind dates, personal ads and other dating sites but where we met was perfect. Neither of us wanted a committed or full-on relationship to start with. Our lives were busy with work and friends and basically we wanted fun, nights out and weekends away and I wanted to be treated like a princess! I'd had some awful experiences with men before and I always seemed to be the one who was helping them and propping them up. I figured it was about time I had some fun instead! It all worked out brilliantly and we are still seeing each other two years on.'

When it comes to dating and wanting to meet new people, it is important to remember that we are all very different. You will want to meet different people to those that perhaps your friends have met online, and therefore you will want to consider different dating sites that meet your needs and criteria rather than those of your friends.

On another note, you must remember that while you may feel super-confident and be bursting with energy and enthusiasm about Internet dating, the people you initially meet online may not be quite as outgoing as you are. Now, one school of thought may dictate that if they are not 'up for it' then you will never get along so what's the point? On the other hand they could just be experiencing a few initial Internet dating insecurities! Give any matches who don't quite provide you with gushing first time emails a second chance – let them get into their stride a bit before you write them off!

# Keeping an open mind

So – you have answered the questions at the beginning of the chapter and you have researched your websites. Chances are that you have chosen more than one website to appear on and that is perfectly acceptable. What you must do however, is try really hard to keep an open mind about the people you bump into during your online love search. Managing your expectations, and those of any potential matches, is really important to ensure a positive Internet dating experience.

Just because someone who has pinged into your inbox doesn't quite tick all your boxes, it does not mean that you should discount them. Put yourself in their place and imagine, just for a few seconds, how *you* would feel if someone deleted your message just because your hair wasn't quite the right colour, or you were a little too short . . . or maybe a year or two too old? Having an idea of who you would like to meet and the kind of relationship you want *is* important, and we have spent a lot of time so far figuring all this out, *but* it is just as important to be fair and kind and generous when people don't quite meet *all* your criteria.

## Case study

Paul, 50, decided to try a mainstream dating site but had a very strict criteria for his 'perfect date'. He said: 'I have always dated beautiful women and saw no reason to stop just because I was 50! I made it clear that I was only interested in meeting women who looked a certain way. I got a lot of flack from other users on the site who felt I was being rude and sexist. As far as I am concerned I was being brutally honest and clear about who I wanted to meet and why. I am a good-looking guy and I wanted a good-looking woman. I am not in a relationship at the moment, but still use dating sites to hook up with women for various work functions. It works for me and I don't care if people don't approve.'

For most of us, to write someone off based on a superficial requirement that you consider to be so important is crazy! If you bumped into someone in the street and they made you laugh or feel like a million dollars but when it came to the crunch and they asked you out, for you to say, 'Oh sorry, I would love to but you are two inches too short . . .' would be ridiculous and a wasted opportunity!

So – keep an open mind, relax the rules a little and who knows who you might bump into out there!

# Staying safe

Staying safe and using some common sense are vital skills to adopt in the Internet dating arena. We already touched on the issue of how much information to sensibly reveal about yourself in the early stages, but one really important element of your Internet dating profile will be your photograph. Depending on the kind of site that you decide to use, and the service terms and conditions of the company that runs the site, you will be given strict guidelines about the type of photo you can use. In the case of a general dating website such as match.com or datingdirect.com you will find that photos range from holiday snaps, to action shots, wedding photos, graduations photos and even those taken for ID cards! There really is a wide range and everyone has a different idea about their best shot. From a personal safety point of view, the best photo to use is one that is clear, recent and decent! Most mainstream sites won't allow anything that remotely resembles obscenity or nudity but others have a more relaxed approach to profile photos. Obviously the site you choose and how much of yourself to reveal (in photos or words) is entirely up to you, but remember that once your photo is published it is there forever and could easily end up just about anywhere – including social networking sites such as Facebook and Twitter.

## Case study

Clare, 29, said she made a huge mistake early in her Internet dating career and regretted it later. She said: 'I sent some saucy photos to a guy I had met online. He seemed genuine and promised he wouldn't send the photos anywhere else. His online name was sexy0078 and he told me the pictures were "for his eyes only". I was *so* naive and should have realised he was up to no good. He sent the photos on to friends and friends of friends, and before I knew it I was tagged in a photo on Facebook. My teenage daughter is on Facebook. There was some fall out and I had to explain which was very awkward.'

Think carefully before you upload, and remember that *anyone* will be able to see your photo.

# Read the small print

If you are paying to subscribe to a dating site then always, always read the small print, particularly the information that relates to cancelling payments from your card or PayPal account. You may be required to give a certain number of days, weeks or even months notice before you can cancel and find yourself firing off emails to customer services on a daily basis to try and sort this out.

As with any contract – read the details and make sure you are fully aware of any terms and conditions. After all, you are paying for a service so you need to be completely clear about what you are getting for your money – and they say romance is dead!

# Summing Up

▨ By now you should have given some proper thought to what it is you want from your online dating experience, and how you are going to take those first steps to surfing for romance.

▨ Remember to research available websites thoroughly, take on board any personal recommendations that apply to you and what you are looking for, and proceed with caution when it comes to making initial contact, giving out details and uploading photos.

▨ It is really worthwhile taking the time to answer the questions at the beginning of the chapter and if it helps, involve a couple of good friends as well to make sure you give honest answers!

▨ Finding the right site, browsing potential matches and uploading your profile is exciting and fun, and with some proper thought, planning and application you will enjoy a positive online dating experience.

# Chapter Seven

# Creating Your Perfect Profile

Now this is when things start to get really exciting . . . and just a little bit scary too if I am honest! When I uploaded my first profile to the very first dating site I found, it was a bit fraught to say the least, but still really exciting. I had never done anything like it before and was convinced that within the week I would have at least two hot dates lined up for my child-free Saturday that was on the horizon!

Well – how wrong I was! Firstly, just trying to resize a photo seemed an almost impossible task and then having to write about myself as well nearly finished me off! I ended up basically writing my CV which was certainly *not* what potential dates wanted to see. These days I help friends knock their profiles into shape to make sure they include all the best bits about themselves and have a good chance of getting some great matches.

In this chapter we will look at how to write a great profile that will get you the right kind of attention, the importance of decent photos and some top tips on how to fine tune your profile to make sure you stand out from the crowd.

Writing 150 words about yourself sounds easy but it really is harder than you think and it is worth having a few goes at it before you upload your final version to your profile. To start with it is very important to be positive and upbeat. Think about what you would like to know about potential matches. For example, we are not really that keen to hear about how someone's ex shafted them, took the kids and all the money and ran off into the sunset with the bloke who was building the extension, are we? It may be a fact of life and the reason that someone is single and now searching for love, but it's not a great opening line!

Avoid overly negative statements that relate to what has happened in your past. After all, this is the future! A new beginning and a chance to wipe the dating and relationship slate clean (save for the accepted level of baggage!). This is your chance to shine and appear confident and optimistic about the rest of your life. The last thing you should be writing in a profile is how much you hate your ex-wife or husband and how life has treated you really badly. Everyone has a story to tell but it's not something that you need to announce on an Internet dating site – trust me!

Some of my early matches were with men who clearly hated women and had plenty to say about how they had been treated by them. Oversharing this kind of information did nothing to endear me to these poor souls and, needless to say, I gave them a very wide berth!

We all have a reason for being single and have sad and difficult stories to tell, but your profile on a dating site is not the place to start these conversations. In the fullness of time there will be an appropriate moment to talk about what has happened before, but for now concentrate on the positive and optimistic side of life.

## Case study

Colin, 48, who signed up for a dating website owned by a major national newspaper said: 'I found that some women on the site I used wanted to moan about their ex-husbands and they were looking for academic, cerebral men rather than a tradesman! I found writing my own profile was difficult because I felt I had to mention that I had children and it was difficult to not sound clichéd when it came to interests and ideas for dates. Although, the profile goes out of the window on a first date anyway because by then you have forgotten what you have written and how many changes you made to it! You have to remember if you have embellished it to try and attract a particular person! It's easy to come unstuck! The answer is to be yourself and be honest and you will be surprised at the results.'

So with so many pitfalls how *do* you get the most out of your online profile? One way to overcome any problems you may have with writing about yourself, is to enlist the help of a friend and see what they have to say about you. How we see ourselves is different to how others see us, and we tend to play down our strengths and focus far more on our weaknesses – particularly when it comes to trying to attract the opposite sex. It is very easy to fall into the trap of looking at what we lack rather than what we have, and a good friend will do the opposite – taking your strengths and attractive qualities and creating a description that is honest and fair but most importantly, well balanced.

Perhaps if you and a single friend are both thinking of giving online dating a try you could write each other's profiles and see who has the best results?

Writing about yourself is tricky and although reading other people's profiles is a good way to find out what other people are saying about themselves, not everyone is entirely honest and things often get embellished, exaggerated or simply made up in the attempt to win the heart of someone else. Therefore, when you are checking out other profiles, remember not all that glitters is necessarily gold, and don't fall into the trap of thinking that everyone else on the site is better than you, sexier than you or more interesting than you, because that's just not the case!

# Why honesty *is* the best policy

It is true that you can be whoever you desire on the Internet. You can shave a few years off your age, a few pounds off your weight and invent the persona of a superhero if you really want to. It might make you feel better for a short time, and maybe a little more in control, but ultimately when you hook up with an enthusiastic downhill skier who has a PhD in astrophysics and a penchant for clubbing and in reality you prefer a walk in the park, have a couple of A levels and like The Carpenters – you may come unstuck!

Whether you decide to create a full-on dishonest fantasy profile or simply make a few 'minor' tweaks in an effort to appear more attractive and marketable, you need to be acutely aware that – guess what? Loads of other people are doing exactly the same thing.

If you met someone in your local library, struck up a conversation and got to know each other, would you feel the need to lie to them? Wouldn't you feel that the very fact you had even had a conversation means there is already a bit of chemistry lurking there under the awkwardness?

To lie online or not to lie online – *that* is the question but if you are hoping to find a proper relationship from your endeavours rather than some cyberspace fantasy, it is far more beneficial to be as honest as you can. This doesn't mean you have to tell everyone everything straight away, but it does mean that if you are 35 then *say* you are 35, and if you can't stand going to the cinema then make it clear. If you don't start as you mean to go on then your relationship will be built on untruths and tall stories – and that is *no* way to create a future with someone.

---

### Case study

Jill, 40, started Internet dating when she was first divorced in 2002. With a busy life already in place with work and her teenage children, Jill thought that all she wanted was some online 'fun' with a single man.

She said: 'That was really what I set out to find so I posted a provocative picture of myself on a particular website, and made up a name. I said that I was looking for intimate online fun and chats on a regular basis. At first the virtual 'romance' that I had created was great fun and just what I wanted, but as time went on I realised that actually I was lonely and wanted to meet men to go on dates with. When I suggested this to some of the guys I got short shrift and was told where to get off. I was accused of being dishonest and trying to lure them into a relationship. You have to be honest in your profile – otherwise it's just not playing fair.'

---

The most important rule of creating your profile has to be honesty. If you are Internet dating because you genuinely want to meet someone for a long-term relationship there is little point in being anything other than completely honest with yourself – and your potential dates.

# A picture tells a thousand words

I have always hated having my photograph taken. For someone who has spent 25 years working in the media and taking photos and filming other people from time to time, I always prefer to be behind the camera! Therefore I completely understand why some people just don't want to have to look down that lens!

However, for Internet dating to be successful, enriching and not a complete waste of time, you really need to get over this fear of photography and embrace the fact that there will be people out there in cyberspace who really *like* the look of you!

Your profile photo is really important because it indicates to other users that you are genuinely trying to have a successful Internet dating experience, and you are taking the process seriously. And, of course, it gives potential dates a good idea of what you look like! We all know that the reason we end up with our partners isn't just down to our appearance, but it is good to be able to put a face to a name – especially on the Internet. And remember, profiles with photos get an average of at least ten times more attention than those without.

Internet daters are often accused of uploading photographs that are out of date and bear little or no resemblance to how they look now. I was actually accused of this myself once! I uploaded a photo in April of one year and didn't update it for about six months. During that time I had lost about two stone and did look different, I also had my hair cut short and coloured a different shade. Although it was obviously still me, there were significant differences. Some of my dates were pleasantly surprised – others thought I was trying to con them! It just goes to show that you can't please all of the people all of the time, and that what one person considers attractive may be different to someone else!

The best photos are those that are clear, in focus and taken in good light. Passport or ID photos should be avoided because they just make anyone look like they are wanted for some hideous crime! Self portraits seem to be a popular way of capturing an image of ourselves, but they really don't work either. The best way to get a good photo is for someone else to take it for you. Pictures taken at desks or tables are fine as you end up with a good head and shoulders shot, but a full length picture is often better.

Here are some top tips for getting a great photograph for your profile:

- Don't take your own photo! Self portraits don't work – especially those that are taken in a mirror!

- It may be basic, but make sure your photo is sharp, in focus and clear.

- Enlist the help of a friend or use a tripod and timer.

- Look directly into the camera and smile!

- Pouting, sultry, sexy poses don't really work and can alter the shape of your face. Be natural for the best results!

- Head shots are fine, but full length pictures are better

- A lot of people use holiday snaps, but the days of swimming with the dolphins, showing off your latest catch on a fishing boat, skiing, yachting and posing next to sports cars that you don't actually own are fading fast!

- Your photo should only be of you – it's not really fair to expect potential matches to try and guess which one you are in a group photo!

- If you are going for a head and shoulders shot, make sure your face fills the frame.

- Remember that you will have to upload a low resolution image to the website so don't forget to compress the file before you add it to your profile.

- Black and white might be moody and arty, but full colour always works best.

## What to leave in . . . and out

So you have a fabulous photo and you are now fine-tuning your profile. What are the crucial bits of information to leave in, and what should you not reveal at this stage?

You should give details of your age, interests and hobbies and as much information as you wish to reveal about your occupation. Obviously this depends on what you do for a living, and how much you are allowed to tell people.

Obvious information relating to your address and even the exact area where you live does not need to be included. It is perfectly acceptable to say you live in Oxfordshire without giving the name of the town or village. If you have children it is safer not to identify them online. Never give out your personal phone numbers or email addresses until you are completely happy that the person you are communicating with can be trusted. Most sites forbid this anyway, preferring members to communicate through their own messaging systems and this is the safest way to establish contact.

# Up close and personal . . . dos and donts

Don't be too quick to start using personal email or MSN to stay in touch. Keep things safe by using the site's own systems to start with. Do not send intimate, personal photos to anyone and do not feel pressured into revealing more information than you are comfortable with. If one of your matches is giving you a hard time and contacting you relentlessly then you may need to lay down a few ground rules. If explaining that you don't have time to constantly be online doesn't work, you may need to break off contact with that person and ask for help from the people who run the site.

# Summing Up

- Once your profile and picture is up on a website you will start to receive messages and contact from people who have been matched with you – and after all – this is the whole point!

- At first you may feel a little disappointed at the people who are contacting you or a little overwhelmed by the numbers of people keen to make contact. Try to keep a clear head and don't read too much into the messages you are receiving.

- Remember that Internet dating is an activity that you are engaging in in addition to the rest of your life and it should not become your life! It is easy to get obsessive about checking your inbox for messages and searching for new matches but try and allocate some time each day to doing this, rather than using every spare second of your day.

- Recent research by an American university has revealed that women can identify what they consider to be attractive men online – just by reading their profiles. The study suggests that uglier men who try to level the playing field by using photos that gloss over their worst features are wasting their time. Apparently, good-looking men were able to convey their confidence and attractiveness in their written self-description and women could spot this without even seeing their photograph . . . I will leave it for you to make your own mind up about that one!

# Chapter Eight

# Communicating in Cyberspace . . . and Beyond!

Internet dating is a whole new way of reaching new people and communicating with them. While we are all very comfortable firing off emails to friends, work colleagues and business associates, 'talking' with potential dates is quite different and requires a different approach.

Some email conversations that I have had with people I have met online have been fascinating, articulate and extremely amusing. Others have been difficult, stilted, dull and lacked any kind of engagement or inspiration. These are the conversations that left me cold with no desire to respond or reply.

However, not everyone has the skills required to write a great email or contact message, and while you may want to ignore them, delete them and forget they ever existed, you must remember that there are rules to the game of Internet dating and if you don't play by them you will find yourself in trouble!

For example, if someone was talking to you in a bar, you wouldn't just turn and walk away from them if they bored you would you? There is no reason to do this online either – good manners cost nothing and you wouldn't like it if someone ignored you, so try and be kind and considerate. Just because the person who has chosen to contact you may not be the kind of person you were hoping to meet, it takes a few seconds to send a quick reply saying thanks but no thanks.

# Email etiquette

As in every other area of your life, remember that there are rules when it comes to email. First of all, DON'T SHOUT! There is no need to write an entire email message in capital letters. It's rude and unnecessary. Reply to emails as soon as you are able, or put an out of office note on to say that you are not online all the time and will get back to people as soon as you can. If you are communicating through a website's contact system then put a note on your profile to the same effect.

Try to resist the temptation to cut and paste a thanks but no thanks message onto an email. You may come unstuck if you make a little mistake and people will know what you have done. If you really don't want to stay in touch with someone then just be honest. It's much kinder than ignoring them or leading them on.

Sending attachments can cause problems for some people's email clients, so if you have got to the stage of using your personal email, just check first, especially if you are sending big files.

Once again, unless you are totally comfortable with it don't send intimate photos of yourself via email. They can end up anywhere. Much better to wait until you meet in person before you get up close and personal!

## Case study

Jane, 43, said: 'I was hounded by one man I met online who seemed to have all the time in the world to sit at his computer and fire off emails. He sent me endless photos of him in various poses and at first it was fun. I was busy working and taking care of my children and only really got to go online in the evening once they were in bed. I found it difficult to keep up with his messages and in the end he sent me an email saying he was going to report me to the website we had met on because I was ignoring him. I really wasn't – it was just that he was unemployed and I was flat out all day every day! I tried to explain that I just didn't have time and he sent me an abusive email. I had to block his address in the end.'

# Using social networking and Windows Messenger/Blackberry Messenger

The same rules apply for messaging systems as for email, but these work instantly so you really do need to have your wits about you! Entire conversations are had in real time and can be stored and kept by both parties, so be very sure that you are totally comfortable with what you are saying, and doing.

Webcams have problems all of their own and, once again, images can be captured so be aware! It may seem fun one evening when you have a glass of wine in your hand, but in the cold light of day you may regret how far you went the night before. Once you are in a committed relationship with someone you can trust – that is different – but in the early days it is easy to get caught up in the excitement and intrigue that Internet dating offers and forget that these people you are communicating with are basically strangers.

A good maxim to apply is to think about how much your very best friends know about you and how long it took you to reveal that information to them, and how long you have known them. Would you have told them intimate details about your life within the first few days of knowing them?

Services such as Blackberry Messenger (BBM) are handy, convenient and fun but can take over your life if you are not careful and disciplined about how they are used. It is also very easy for people to be offended if you don't respond to their messages instantly, as this is what they will be expecting. If you don't plan to continue with a conversation then don't start one using instant messaging. Instead stick to email contact as you do have more control over how and when you reply.

## Don't become a stalker – or be stalked!

We have talked a lot about how obsessive Internet dating can be, and this works both ways. If the thought of someone constantly trying to contact you and demand your time makes your blood run cold, then you need to make sure that your own behaviour reflects this. You may well think that you have just met the love of your life and you can't wait to hear from them again. They may or may not feel the same, but this is just the beginning and should be a time of great excitement and anticipation. Don't spoil things by moving things too fast, as this can only lead to disappointment. You have to respect other people's privacy and the time constraints on their lives. Just because they don't respond to you as quickly as you would ideally like, it does not mean that you can constantly bother them, and send them increasingly abrupt, rude and demanding messages.

---

### Case study

Miranda, 38, found that she had to change her mobile number because of a problem she experienced with an Internet dater.

She said: 'I was so naive and if I could give one piece of advice to anyone who is thinking of doing Internet dating, I would say that if you do want to communicate via mobile – get another one. I should have set up a pay as you go phone just for the purpose of Internet dating because I found myself in a ridiculous situation with two men ringing me and texting me while I was trying to work. It was hopeless. In the end things got so bad that I had to change my number and it was really inconvenient. It didn't work out with either of these two men and one in particular really stalked me for several months. I had no choice but to change my number.'

---

# Know when to give up

No matter how hard it is to admit – sometimes things are just not meant to be and we have to be honest with ourselves and others that the time has come to call it a day.

## Case study

For Linda, 50, this proved to be really difficult and when the man she had met online told her he was actually still married and wasn't even available for a relationship her world fell apart. She said: 'I was devastated. For months we had been emailing each other and the messages had got more and more intimate. I trusted him so I didn't see a problem with the way I was behaving and he said such lovely things to me. He told me that he was separated from his wife and that he couldn't believe I hadn't been snapped up by someone already. He said all the right things and he had promised to finally meet up for dinner. The night before he emailed me to say that actually he was married and if I was interested in being his mistress that was fine, but he wasn't ever going to leave his wife. I was stupid for believing him and it knocked my confidence for ages. Even now, a few years on, I have difficulty trusting people. I found it all very difficult to accept and have to confess that I even tried to find out where he lived so that I could go and see him. It was then that I realised it had been me giving out all the information and he had kept things close to his chest.'

Matt, in his mid twenties, had a similar experience.

## Case study

Matt said, 'I met a girl online and we were getting along really well. She was keen to meet up so I said yes because I don't believe in dragging things out. When we met she was nice enough but there was no real chemistry there. I suggested that we just stay friends and she was furious at this idea. She pestered me, found me on Facebook and tried to make things really difficult. I know she found it hard that I basically rejected her, but I could have led her on, used her for sex and then dumped her. Surely that would have been far worse. People need to understand that sometimes things don't work out and that's that.'

# No means no

Ultimately we all have to accept that when someone tells us they don't want to contact us again or meet us then they mean it and we have to respect that. The Americans have an excellent and healthy approach to the dating scene, and although our cultures are different and as a nation we tend to be far more reserved, in many ways their approach to finding a partner is a good one.

They treat their dating experiences in a business-like and very transparent way, by making it clear to the people they are seeing that they are doing just that – seeing a few people at a time before they decide on who is right for them. Everyone knows where they stand, and although it may seem to strip away any of the romance of dating, it is practical, sensible and honest. I am sure that it is not 100% water tight and that problems do arise, but the method and basic premise is a good one. It's a bit like the old saying about 'not putting all your eggs in one basket'!

One of the major advantages of the Internet dating phenomenon is the very fact that we have lots and lots of people to choose to go on dates with. You will not hit it off with everyone you meet, so it begs the question as to why we would concentrate all of our efforts in one place. By spreading our net as wide as possible and meeting new, different people on a regular basis we increase our chances of meeting the right person and being in control of our dating career.

# Summing Up

- Taking time to be polite to the people you meet on your Internet dating journey takes only a few minutes, but will mean a lot to anyone who has contacted you. Even if you don't want to pursue a friendship or relationship with them, they are effectively in the same boat as you and deserve the respect that you would demand from them.

- Of course, we are all different and just because you behave appropriately, unfortunately not everyone will behave in the same way so you need to be prepared for that and put your own rules and boundaries in place.

- Internet dating should be fun, exciting and intriguing and can literally change your life. Just treat the experience with respect and remember that it is all about people's lives, desires and hopes for the future.

# Chapter Nine

# The First Date

And this is what it's *all* about! You have been exchanging messages or emails for a few weeks, months or maybe even longer and you have both got to the point where you are comfortable about the idea of actually meeting in person!

The crucial thing to remember here is that you must *both* feel comfortable with meeting up. I remember vividly my first ever Internet date – and not because it was good unfortunately! The man I was planning to meet lived on the Isle of Man and was prepared to make a long trip to where I lived in order to meet. We had only ever emailed, had never spoken on the phone and if I am honest, although I was very excited, I was also very nervous. He came equipped with copies of bank statements, a photo of his house and a proposal of marriage! All a bit much for a first date and perhaps an extreme example, but it's completely true!

I was swept up with the excitement and potential romance of it all but the reality was that he had received orders from his parents to marry quickly or risk losing his inheritance! Not an ideal first date that's for sure!

I urge you to think carefully before you meet, but on the other hand don't drag things out for too long either.

## What's the plan?

Have you got a perfect first date in mind? Do you imagine your eyes meeting and falling in love at first sight? Are you thinking about a stroll in the park? Chatting over a latte in an intimate coffee shop? Or something more cerebral such as an afternoon spent in an art gallery or museum?

Well I have had *all* of these brilliant ideas for a first date and have done all of them as well as ice skating, yachting and wine tasting! However, things have a nasty habit of not quite working out the way you planned, so it's a very good idea to have some flexibility built into your plans.

Most people I spoke to when I was researching this book agree that the best dates they have been on were the most simple. By trying too hard to impress you can find yourself in awkward and potentially stressful situations, so keep the first date short, sweet and simple. A coffee, or drink in a local pub or bar is straightforward and an easy expectation to manage. In time there will be plenty of opportunities to do other things and explore interests. This is the time when you need to concentrate on getting to know each other. If you indulge in a date that is complex or too unusual then this will simply serve as a distraction and you may come away from the date wondering if you are any further forward and know anything about each other at all!

People often make the mistake of pulling out all the stops to try and impress someone on a first date, only to be shot down in flames when the expensive meal in a fancy restaurant fails to hide the fact that they have lied about their age! Dating can be a disappointing experience and something that leaves you with a heavy heart and a real feeling of dread when it comes to future dates. To avoid these negative feelings, suggest dates that are pleasant but perfectly manageable and that will provide both of you with plenty of chances to ask questions and get to know each other.

## Case study

Sally, 35, said: 'One of my first dates was with a man called Jason. We had been flirting and chatting online and he just came to my house one afternoon. I thought all my Christmases had come at once! He pulled up outside in a Porsche and came to the door with a magnum of champagne and some strawberries. It all got very out of hand and we ended up sleeping together. His performance was impaired by the alcohol but he blamed me and said I was too fat for him. It was horrendous and I really regretted it. He never contacted me again but I felt used and worthless.'

# Where to meet and who to tell

This is where the rules of blind dates have their place, and make no mistake – you may well have been conversing via email but this is still effectively a blind date. Here are some key points to remember when you are embarking on your Internet dates:

▧ Arrange to meet in a public place that you know will be busy.

▧ Make the date during the day if possible rather than an evening. From my experiences, Saturday morning coffee or Saturday afternoon tea work best. That way you have the option to cut it short on the basis that you have plans for the rest of the day, if things don't quite go according to plan.

▧ Always, always tell at least one person where you are going, what time you are meeting and some basic details about your date.

▧ Always keep your mobile switched on and to hand.

- Make a plan with a good friend to call you or text you at a certain time. Decide on a code word to use so that if your date is abysmal you can let your friend know and have an 'emergency' to deal with. This may sound harsh but it is a good back up plan. Some dates I had just ended quickly, because it was clear we hadn't clicked and we were not likely to for whatever reason. However, on a couple of occasions when I felt like leaping from a second floor ladies' toilet window to escape, the code word system worked brilliantly and meant I could make my excuses without risking injury!

# Back up and back out plans

So – there you are staring at your inbox and the offer of a date pops in. Hurrah! Success! This is what you have been waiting for and you intend to relish the moment and have the best date of your life! You immediately start planning your outfit and potentially the rest of your life!

*Easy tiger!*

Remember this is a *first* date and it may or may not work out so try to maintain a measured approach to this event in your life, because the way you feel today might well change by this time tomorrow. I had many experiences like this when I got extremely excited about a date and then had serious misgivings and wanted to back out. I have to confess that on at least two occasions I turned up, saw the person I was meeting across the road and just couldn't do it. So I walked on by. I never heard from those people again – so for the record this is a public apology for some appalling dating behaviour.

So why did I back out? Mostly because I thought I just couldn't face another rejection or spending my precious child-free time with someone whose main passion in life was Chelsea FC. It was mean, unkind and cruel but I just got cold feet – plain and simple. And to add balance I was stood up on more than one occasion so I got my just desserts!

If the night before the big date you suddenly get struck down with a case of the first date nerves and just can't comprehend meeting this stranger, then the best option you have available is to let them know – especially if you know that they are planning to travel from some distance. Explain how you feel and just leave it at that. Some things are just not meant to happen and only you know what you can handle and what you can't.

# Good manners

Don't leave people standing on street corners. It makes you feel horrible and people look at you as if you have just landed from another planet. It also screams of being stood up! If you are not going to make it then let the other person know.

When you do meet, if they don't come up to your expectations have a coffee, a quick chat and just make it clear that you only have an hour to spare. There is no need to be cruel or unkind. One man once told me that he was hoping I would look younger in real life than my profile photo, and was bitterly disappointed as he didn't want a 'mumsy' girlfiend! I almost tipped his pint over him but resisted the temptation and left – quickly. There was no need for this level of sheer rudeness and it really did upset me.

---

### Case study

Miranda, 38, said: 'I had a date with a man who assumed that I was going back to his place and had even ordered a large bottle of wine and a cab to get us there. I was genuinely disgusted and appalled by this assumption. Quite apart from the fact that I would never go back to anyone's house on a first date, he was extremely rude when I told him I wasn't interested and asked me if I was a lesbian! Pathetic!'

---

# When things don't work out

It is always a shame when you build something up in your mind, only to experience a disappointing first date. It's easy to say, but it's really hard not to dwell on what has happened. Try not to overanalyse. At the end of the day this was just a date – nothing more – and there will be more dates just around the corner. It is very unusual to find the person you are going to spend the rest of your life so quickly, so don't be disheartened and don't start doubting yourself or blaming yourself.

If you feel you can't face another date for a while, that is perfectly normal and maybe you do need to give yourself some time to think about things, but look on this as a positive event in your life as it will ultimately lead you to the person who you will have a lasting relationship with. Although I had lots of Internet dates and I have this book all about that, I didn't meet my partner online. However, I do not regret any of the Internet dates I had because they helped me get to know myself better and made me realise who I really wanted to be with and what their most important qualities should be.

# Summing Up

- First dates are exciting, fraught and anxious, but try hard to manage your expectations.

- Anyone who says they really don't care if the person they are meeting likes them or not is a liar. We all care what other people think of us and to go into dating with that attitude will not help you because you are effectively saying that you couldn't care less anyway. If that's how you feel then you have to ask yourself why you are even bothering with Internet dating.

- Keep a clear head, be positive, feel good about yourself and just think of this as one of many interesting dates to come, and trust me – you will soon have loads of great dating stories to share!

# Chapter Ten

# Living the Dating Dream or Having a Complete Nightmare?

By this stage you will probably have got to grips with Internet dating and have had a few dates that you can talk about with your friends and take experiences from that will help you decide on the kind of relationship you want, and the kind of people you would like to connect with online.

Perhaps you have been lucky enough to have enjoyed a string of excellent dates with people who you really connected with, or perhaps you have a couple of stalkers who just won't leave you alone. Whatever your experiences, good and bad, now is the time to take a step back.

It could be that you have signed up with more than one website and that what you thought you originally wanted from the experience has changed in some way. Well this is a good opportunity to have a look at what has happened so far and see how you feel about things.

Start by answering the questions below to try and find out where you are with your Internet dating.

## Evaluating your experiences:

- How long have you been Internet dating for?
- How many websites are you using on a regular basis?
- How much time are you spending each day/week/month on Internet dating?

- How successful has the matching process been for you?

- How many dates have you been on?

- Are you planning to see anyone again?

- How do you feel about yourself? Confident and attractive, or are you lacking in self-esteem?

- Have you had any bad Internet dating experiences?

There are no right or wrong answers to these questions, but answering them will give you a really good idea of how you should now move forward. I notched up an impressive 80 dates over the course of about 12 years, and few of them could be described as completely successful! However, those experiences taught me a lot about myself and sent me back to the dating drawing board on more than one occasion to rewrite my profile, change my websites or upload a different photo. It really is a learning curve and there is no right or wrong way to do it. If you want to have a few dates each week you will have to invest more time than someone who is only hoping for one or two dates a month, but really the amount of time you invest in the search for online romance is only limited by your time and capacity to go out and have dates.

If you have found that you are spending a lot of time online but not actually getting very far then perhaps you should consider either changing websites for a while, or actually being bold and making the first move to ask someone out. Otherwise you could be waiting forever! Although it can be a bit scary to have to be the one to take the bull by the horns, it could be the best move you ever make and let's face it – what's the worst that can happen? Okay so they may say no, so just move on to the next one! A good friend once told me that dating is a numbers game – and that's very true! With the amount of people now in cyberspace looking for love, there are no excuses for lining up a few dates and seeing how you get on.

Perhaps it's a good time to revisit your profile and photo and see if a few tweaks or updates here and there could make a difference to your success with matches. Perhaps you are now feeling a bit more confident than you were a few months ago so you are now more able to sing your praises and talk positively about yourself. Perhaps you really have learned a bit more about yourself as well. After all, I consider Internet dating to have been an important part of my personal development plan and you should too. It isn't all plain sailing but you do learn a lot about what you will tolerate, what you are interested in and, most importantly, what makes you happy.

# Keeping in touch or not

I may not have met my partner through the Internet dating scene, but to my surprise I did make some good friends who I am still in touch with. It was clear to both of us when we met that there was no relationship on the horizon, but we have become friends and have actually supported each other with our quest for true love!

---

## Case study

Suzi, 36, had the same experience. She said: 'I wanted a boyfriend – plain and simple – but actually it turns out that what I needed was a good friend. My ex-partner and I had divorced and I had moved away to a new town where I knew nobody. When a relationship breaks down you tend to lose friends as well so I was at rock bottom. Looking back on it, a relationship at that time would have been no good for me. When I met Brian I didn't fancy him and he didn't fancy me but we had both been through the mill and found we had lots in common. We have grown to be great friends and spend a lot of time together. He was just what I needed. I very nearly didn't go on that date with Brian because my confidence was in bits at the time, but I am so glad that I did!'

---

Staying in touch with someone you may have been out with a few times can work, unless they want something that you don't. In that case it is just far kinder to back out at this stage rather than keep someone dangling with the false hope that one day maybe you will get it together.

If you are completely convinced they are not relationship material, however difficult it may be, just tell them. That way you can both deal with it and move forward – onto the next date!

# The good . . . the bad . . . and the ugly

There is no getting away from the fact that unless you are somehow blessed by the mysterious divine goddess of dating – there will be bad and ugly dates as well as good ones! However, try at all times to keep your sense of humour. If you don't you will find you become eaten up by negative experiences and this will really hamper any efforts you are making to move forward in your life. After all, the people you meet along the way are transient in your life – they will come and they will go. Some may hang around for a while – maybe longer – but by and large you never have to see them again so don't let them affect your life in a way that will impact on your self-confidence.

Good dates are always the best – obviously – and the idea is that you have more of these than the bad and the ugly, but ultimately dating is an experience that creates a myriad of different emotions and feelings so you will have good days and bad as well as good dates and bad ones. Try to always focus on the positive and good dates and treat the others with good humour – if you can! Everything that you go through as a single person and an Internet dater will shape the rest of your life. So keep the negative stuff to a minimum, stay positive and then you will attract positive events into your life as well as positive, optimistic people.

# Dealing with disappointment

Disappointment is a tricky business! Imagine how you would feel if a good friend or relative let you down badly, or someone at work? You would be justified in feeling down and disillusioned with their behaviour and the way they have treated you. This is because these people have been in your life for a long time and you have invested heavily in your relationships with them. It is only right for you to feel personally wounded and let down by them.

However, although dating is an emotional roller coaster and, as we know, it is very easy to get very involved with someone early on, just remember that you have not had the time or opportunity to invest too much in these new people in your life just yet. Therefore, although you will feel a little down if things don't work out just remember that you have known these people for a tiny, miniscule amount of time and in reality you don't know them, and they don't know you – at all.

My Internet dating support network (in other words my good friends!) would always immediately tell me that it was their loss when yet another man let me down, criticised me or just rejected me. My current partner now says he would like to shake every last one of them by the hand because if they hadn't turned out to be non-runners we may never have got together!

So you see – even the bad and difficult dates you have can translate into a success story of one sort or another!

# Celebrating success

Of course, the very best case scenario is that you read this book, take on board all the tried and tested tips, absorb some of the case studies and get out there and nail Internet dating! I truly hope this happens and that you do find love online – no matter how long it takes.

There are no right or wrong ways to date online, I have simply shared with you my own experiences and those of people who I have met along the way, in the hope that this will help to guide you on your own Internet dating journey.

The experience has undoubtedly enriched my life and even though I encountered a few undesirables along the way who were often quite unkind to me, I forgive them all because I am now in the privileged position of knowing myself really well, and having met some really interesting and unusual people who all have different stories to tell about their lives and how they became single. They weren't all honest but then there is a reason why we cover things up and I hope that as they got on with their lives they all found people who they could be honest with and who they felt good enough for.

Success at Internet dating can be measured in a couple of ways. The obvious way is by the very nature of the fact that you may well now be in a relationship and deliriously happy, or you may well be enjoying having a few dates every month and positively embracing the single life and all it has to offer!

Another way of measuring success is through personal growth and your own happiness levels. I had many years of being single and most of those were very happy times and I thoroughly made the most of them. Yes I had dates and if I am honest I was probably always hoping to find a lovely boyfriend, but along the way I had a blast and I look back on those days with great affection.

Internet dating gets a lot of bad press, but I know many people who have found love online. In fact at the end of 2010 my own cousin, Alison, met the love of her life, Guy, online and we all enjoyed a fabulous family wedding in the autumn of 2011. I wish them all the love and luck in the world and I think the fact that they met online, defied the odds and proved that love can be found and flourishes in cyberspace speaks volumes about how Internet dating is developing all the time. Far from being a guilty secret to be hidden from friends and family, it is fast becoming a sophisticated and finely-tuned portal for everything from casual dates to marriage proposals, and should be considered to be the modern way to meet people and find love.

I truly hope that you find this book useful and that you enjoy the excitement and intrigue that Internet dating has to offer. Next time you are nursing a cup of coffee and listening to Steve Wright's Sunday Love Songs on BBC Radio 2, grab that laptop and start writing your own love story!

There's a lot of love to be found out there in cyberspace, and I would like to wish you good luck in finding love online!

# Help List

### eHarmony.co.uk

This site has 1.5 million users and is for people who are serious about finding their life partner. It is free to browse and £34.99 a month to join.

### Loveandfriends.com

This site has around 120,000 users and is for people who would like to develop friendships as well as relationships. Registration and basic membership is free and monthly full membership is £16.95 a month.

### Match.com

Membership runs into millions and match.com also owns Dating Direct. Another related site, matchaffinity.com, asks members to fill in an in-depth compatibility report. This site is free to create a profile and browse and membership costs £29.99 a month.

### Mysinglefriend.com

This site has over a million users, and a friend writes a profile for their single friend. It is free to add profile information and to browse and receive emails but £22 a month for membership.

### parship.co.uk

This site has 2.6 million users and is aimed at professional people aged 30 and over who are looking for a long-term relationship. It is free to browse and membership is £39.90 a month.

### zoosk.com

Eight million singles from across the world use this site every day through a Facebook application. Attracts younger people and is free to join, full membership costs £18.95 a month.

# Book List

## Love Life Live Life

By Sue Stone available from www.suestone.com
Author of 'Love Life, Live Life' and a Transformational Leader and Coach, Sue Stone is known in the media as the UK's happiest and most positive person. Founder of the Sue Stone Foundation, Sue's amazing positivity and energy has infiltrated the lives of thousands, with wonderful results both at home and in the workplace.

## The Little Book of Internet Dating

By Tom Collins, published by Michael O'Mara Books Limited and available from Amazon.

## Everyone's Guide to Online Dating

By Shimrit Elisar published by How To Books Ltd and available from Amazon.

## Online Dating for Dummies

By Dr. Judith Silverstein M.D. and Michael Lasky J.D

Need2Know

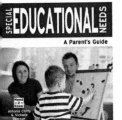

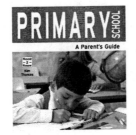
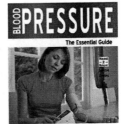
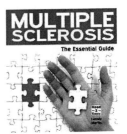